SWANS

Text & drawing page 4 copyright © 1995 by Dafila Scott
Photographs copyright © 1995 by

Front Cover © Laurie Campbell
Back Cover © Jim Brandenburg (Minden Pictures)
Page 1   © Kit Breen
Page 6   © William Paton (NHPA)
Page 9   © Frans Lanting (Minden Pictures)
Page 10   © Janos Jurka
Page 12   © Philippa Scott (NHPA)
Page 13   © Laurie Campbell (NHPA)
Page 14   © Roger Tidman (FLPA)
Page 17   © Roger Wilmshurst (FLPA)
Page 18   © Frank Schneidermeyer (Oxford Scientific Films)
Page 19   © E & D Hosking (FLPA)
Page 21   © Tony Howard (NHPA)
Page 22   © William Paton (NHPA)
Page 25   © Melvin Grey (NHPA)
Page 26   © Lady Philippa Scott
Page 29   © A R Hamblin (FLPA)
Page 30   © Orion Press (NHPA)
Page 33   © Rich Kirchner (NHPA)
Page 33   © Rich Kirchner (NHPA)
Page 34   © Colin Baxter

Page 37   © Jim Brandenburg (Minden Pictures)
Page 38   © Eileen C Rees (Wildfowl & Wetlands Trust)
Page 40   Top © Dafila Scott
Page 40   Bottom © Chris & Jo Knights (Nature Photographers Ltd)
Page 43   © Colin Baxter
Page 44   © E & D Hosking (FLPA)
Page 47   © Jim Brandenburg (Minden Pictures)
Page 49   © Roger Hosking (FLPA)
Page 50   © Babs & Bert Wells (Oxford Scientific Films)
Page 53   © Eric Soder (NHPA)
Page 54   © Daniel J Cox (Natural Exposures)
Page 55   © Dafila Scott
Page 57   © Robin Bush (Nature Photographers Ltd)
Page 58   © Edward Robinson (Oxford Scientific Films)
Page 60   © Manfred Danegger (NHPA)
Page 61   © Manfred Danegger (NHPA)
Page 62   © Scott Camazine (Oxford Scientific Films)
Page 65   © Janos Jurka
Page 66   © Robin Bush (Nature Photographers Ltd)
Page 67   © Mike Birkhead (Oxford Scientific Films)
Page 68   © Janos Jurka

Edited by Mike Rensner
Designed by Colin Baxter
Printed in Singapore

95   96   97   98   99   5   4   3   2   1

Library of Congress Cataloging-in-Publication Data

Scott, Dafila.
   Swans / by Dafila Scott.
      p. cm. -- (World life library)
   Includes bibliographical references (p. 72).
   ISBN 0-89658-320-1
   1. Swans.   I. Title.   II. Series.
QL696. A52S325   1995
598.4' 1--dc20   95-32902
                                                          CIP

Distributed in Canada by Raincoast Books, 8680 Cambie Street, Vancouver, B. C. V6P 6M9

Published by Voyageur Press, Inc.
123 North Second Street, P. O. Box 338, Stillwater, MN 55082 U. S. A.
612-430-2210, fax 612-430-2211

Please write or call, or stop by, for our free catalog of natural history publications. Our toll-free number
to place an order or to obtain a free catalog is 800-888 WOLF (800-888-9653)

Educators, fundraisers, premium and gift buyers, publicists, and marketing managers: Looking for
creative products and new sales ideas? Voyageur Press books are available at special discounts when
purchased in quantities, and special editions can be created to your specifications. For details contact the
marketing department.

SWANS

Dafila Scott

Voyageur Press

Contents

Swans usually pair for life, or until the death of their partner. These North American Trumpeter Swans are the largest of the swans.

The Nature of Swans

In Tchaikovsky's ballet, *Swan Lake*, Siegfried falls in love with the beautiful Odette, who must spend part of each day as a swan. To him she is lovelier than any of the girls brought before him as possible brides and he vows his undying love for her. This resolve fails only when he is tricked by the evil magician into thinking that Odile, the magician's daughter, is Odette. When the real Odette appears and Siegfried realises the deception, a storm arises – in the happier version, the spell is broken, and the couple live happily ever after.

In legends and myths, swans represent beauty, purity and fidelity. It is easy to see why, for swans combine grace with elegance. Their whiteness represents purity. Fidelity suggests strength of character. But what are swans really like?

In real life, swans possess many of the characteristics that we find admirable. We now know that they usually pair for life, or until the death of their partner. They are family birds, the parents look after their cygnets even after fledging, and defend them fiercely against predators and potential competitors. Swans are traditional in their habits; the migratory swans usually return to the same breeding and wintering places every year, flying thousands of kilometres. Parents pass on the knowledge of these sites to their offspring.

But it is a mistake to think of swans in moral terms. If they are faithful and caring in their behaviour it is likely to be for reasons of self-interest. Like all animals they are products of evolution, and natural selection favours those individuals which leave the most offspring and survive best. So how can we explain the fidelity of swans in these terms? Recent studies of the lives of individual swans have begun to show how these 'admirable' charcteristics may have evolved, and how they are interwoven with the swans' large size and with their ecology. Being so large has a number of consequences. It means that individuals of either sex cannot breed more than once per year because the young take a long time to grow, and males cannot afford to defend territories large enough for more than one female. So fathers benefit by helping with parental care, and monogamy becomes the best strategy. For the swans, long-term monogamy has considerable benefits in terms of increased breeding success.

Swans are among the largest flying birds with a ratio of wing area to body weight that is so low that they are approaching the limits of airworthiness – theoretically they should be incapable of flying. So how do they achieve lift-off? First, like airliners, they need long runways for taking off and landing. Second, they must fly fairly fast, and so find it difficult to make tight manoeuvres.

Swans are the largest of the waterfowl (Anseriformes), a group which also includes geese and ducks. Swans were probably one of the earlier groups to evolve, since they share common features with both ducks and geese, including webbed feet, wide spatulate bills, and legs set well back on the body for increased swimming efficiency. Their origins are still obscure, but swan-like birds may have existed for as long as 80 million years. Fossils of birds are notoriously rare because their light air-filled bones are easily crushed, and any remains are usually fragmentary. The earliest waterfowl fossils date from the Eocene period (40-50 million years ago). By the time humans evolved, swans were well established. One fossil that has survived is that of a giant extinct Maltese swan, dating from the Pleistocene period, which was discovered and described in the second half of the nineteenth century. This bird, weighing about 16kg (35.3lb), was rather larger than any existing swan. Unfortunately we do not know whether it could fly, or whether it was black or white. Another swan, the New Zealand Swan, probably died out in the sixteenth century at the hands of Polynesian colonists. Its bones have been found in the middens of these people, who also hunted the now extinct giant moas of New Zealand.

All swans except Coscoroba Swans belong to the genus *Cygnus*, so named after the Greek hero, Cygnus, who was transformed into a swan as he mourned the death of his friend Phaethon. The unfortunate Phaethon was struck by a thunderbolt from above and drowned in the river Po, after trying unsuccessfully to drive his father Helios' sun-chariot.

From the earliest times, swans have been associated with the gods, and sometimes their sacred nature has protected them from harm by people. However, swans have been hunted and otherwise exploited in many parts of the world throughout history, and in some cases it is only quite recently that action has been taken to restore the balance in their favour.

Swan Species

Most scientists recognise eight species of swans worldwide. In the northern hemisphere there are five: Mute Swans, Bewick's Swans, Whistling Swans (sometimes known as Tundra Swans), Whooper Swans and Trumpeter Swans. In the southern hemisphere, there are three: Black Swans of Australia, and Black-necked and Coscoroba Swans of South America (though Mute Swans have been introduced into Australia and South Africa). All are considered separate species except for Bewick's and Whistling Swans which, since the differences between them are slight, are usually classified as one species *Cygnus columbianus*. In this case the species as a whole is well described as the Tundra Swan, since these birds nest only on the arctic tundra. However, the two sub-species inhabit different continents with little overlap in range and a small amount of interbreeding where they meet. They are usually distinguishable in the field, so it is convenient to retain the distinction.

Bewick's and Whistling Swans are closely related to Whooper and Trumpeter Swans. These four characteristically have powerful trumpeting or bugling calls, made possible by the special anatomy of their windpipes, which are all long and convoluted. Mute, Black and Black-necked Swans form another though less closely related group, all having quieter calls and simple windpipes. Coscoroba Swans are not closely related to any other swan species.

Coscoroba Swans

Coscoroba Swans are the smallest of the swans and the most duck-like with their wide red bills and extra feathering on the face. (All the other swans have bare skin extending from the bill in a wedge going back to the eye.) Coscorobas also differ from the other swans in having strikingly patterned cygnets. Unlike the uniform grey down of the others, young Coscorobas hatch with a coat of black and white down, similar to that of downy

A group of Whooper Swans on a lake in Sweden.

tree-ducks (Dendrocygnini). Coscorobas use more down to line their nests than the other swans and, having shorter, broader wings, they are also able to take off directly from the surface of the water, without having to run to gain flight speed. Unusually, they have black tips to their primary wing feathers. They also have pink legs and feet, while the other swans usually have black legs and feet.

The geographical range of Coscoroba Swans in South America extends from Tierra del Fuego and the Falkland Islands in the south, to the north of Uruguay and into Brazil in the north. The largest concentrations are in southern Chile and Argentina. While the central part of the population is mostly sedentary, remaining in one area throughout the year, depending on conditions, the southernmost breeding birds migrate north for the winter. The total number of Coscoroba Swans has never been counted systematically, but estimates suggest that there may be somewhere between 10,000 and 25,000 individuals.

A pair of Coscoroba Swans preening.

They were given their name by the South American Indians as it reminded them of the swans' call, a slightly hoarse, whistling, burbling 'cos-cor-ro-oa'. When a pair perform a duet, the call of the male is usually higher-pitched than that of the female but otherwise the sexes are similar, except in size, males being around 20% heavier than females.

Mute Swans

Mute Swans, with their bright orange-red bill and black knob, are familiar to many

Mute Swans raise their wings above their backs in a spectacular
'busking' display, used to intimidate opponents. Male swans or 'cobs' tend to perform
this display in a more exaggerated fashion than females or 'pens'.

people who regularly visit their local ponds or waterways. These swans have a long history of domestication and semi-domestication in Europe, and now often live in close proximity to people. They are well adapted for life in the water with legs set towards the back of the body, and anyone who has watched them out of the water will know that this gives them a characteristically awkward gait. Mute Swans sometimes exceed Trumpeter Swans in weight and so may count among the heaviest flying birds, although they are not so large in linear measurements. They accentuate their size with the spectacular 'busking' display, raising their wings high above their backs in silent menace. Mute Swans are notoriously aggressive in the breeding season and if you approach a nest too closely you risk a blow from a very powerful wing. Even swan research workers have suffered fractured bones! In flight their wingbeats are accompanied by a regular whistling sound, making them louder than the wingbeats of the other swans. Unlike the others, Mute Swans do not call in flight. On land or water, they usually restrict themselves to quiet snorts and grunts, though cygnets will squeak in high-pitched voices if they become separated from their parents, and all Mute Swans will hiss loudly in reptilian manner if threatened. Like the other swans, males are larger than females (35% heavier) and usually have a larger black knob on the bill. Both sexes develop larger knobs and brighter red bills during the breeding season. Young birds usually have grey bills and small knobs. For the first year, youngsters are also characterized by their grey-brown plumage, which becomes more patchy as white feathers grow through. Although individuals can become completely white within a year, sometimes grey feathers are still apparent after fifteen months or more.

Some Mute Swans develop white instead of grey plumage as youngsters and have pale pinkish legs. They are called Polish Mutes, as they were originally more common in eastern Europe. These birds are genetically distinct from normal Mute Swans, and seem at first to be at a disadvantage. Because the cygnets are white they provoke aggression from their own parents and can be chased off the territory before their grey siblings. Then, once separated from their family, they are less camouflaged and more vulnerable to predation and to competition with other swans. However, there seems to be a compensating advantage. Female Polish swans appear adult sooner than normal Mutes and tend to pair and breed sooner. Polish swans may, in the past, have had the added advantage of being avoided by hunters who preferred to kill grey youngsters for the table.

Mute Swans are the most successful of all swans in terms of numbers. The Palearctic population alone is now thought to comprise about 500,000 individuals. These birds are distributed throughout Europe and Central Asia, and numbers are thought to have increased by 30% since the 1970s. In Central Asia, Mute Swans are concentrated in the Black Sea area, the Volga River delta in the Caspian Sea and in Kazakhstan. In Europe they are concentrated in the Scandinavian-Baltic area and in Central Europe, the latter population expanding eastwards towards the Black Sea. Studies suggest that a small amount of interchange regularly occurs between neighbouring populations, though some populations, particularly those breeding in the south of the range, are mostly sedentary, remaining in their territories throughout the year when possible. Birds breeding in the north of the range, or in the cold continental interior, migrate south to areas of open water for the winter. Some birds also move long distances to special moulting areas. Swans, geese and ducks are unusual among birds in shedding all their flight feathers at one time, so that for a period of four to six weeks, they cannot fly. This makes them vulnerable to predators and so they commonly move to large lakes, estuaries or sheltered coastal waters during these times.

The early domestication of Mute Swans makes it difficult to determine the extent of their original range, though they probably came from Central Europe and Asia, and may have been introduced in countries to the north and west. They have also been introduced to other continents. In North America the population now numbers around 7,900, and in Australia and South Africa there are stable but smaller populations.

Black-necked Swans

Like Coscoroba Swans, Black-necked Swans are inhabitants of South America, their range covering much the same ground as the Coscoroba. They breed in the Falkland

Islands, Tierra del Fuego, Argentina, the southern half of Chile, Uruguay, and wetlands in south-east Brazil and Paraguay. Although no complete count has ever been made, it is estimated that 100,000 swans inhabit the South American mainland, the largest concentrations being in Argentina, and about 2,500 inhabit the Falkland Islands. As with Coscorobas, Black-necked Swans breeding in the southern parts of the range migrate north during winter. New studies will soon help to discover exactly where they pass the winter. Initial results show that the swans may move long distances, not only with the changing seasons, but also with changing conditions. A major drought in the austral summer of 1988-9, which affected Argentina, Brazil and Uruguay, forced the Black-necked Swans to move south to Chile where observers recorded the arrival of ringed swans at the Rio Cruces Nature Sanctuary.

Black-necked Swans, in common with Mute and Black Swans, sometimes carry their downy young on their backs.

Living on large lakes and marshes, Black-necked Swans spend little time on land, and, like Mute Swans, are ungainly on land, with legs set well back on their bodies for efficient swimming. In common with Mute Swans, they have a fleshy lobe at the base of the bill, but in their case it is a striking bright red against a grey-blue bill, and it may develop several bulges. As with the other swans, males are slightly larger than females (30% heavier) and may have larger red lobes on the bill, but otherwise they are similar in appearance. Black-necked Swans are quite vocal and, when displaying aggressively, make a wheezy whistling call, usually in duet with their partner.

Black Swans

The idea of a Black Swan was so alien to seventeenth-century Europeans that they refused to believe in such a bird when reports of its discovery first came in. The discovery was made by a Dutch navigator, Willem de Vlaming, in western Australia in 1697. When the first Black Swans arrived in Europe, people were fascinated. The Empress Josephine kept several on her pond at Malmaison. But the distinction by plumage colour is superficial. Black Swans are closely related to the other species. Again males are slightly larger than females (20% heavier) though otherwise similar. In both sexes the greater wing coverts and scapular feathers are broadened and curled, giving the birds a spectacular black, ruffled mantle which is raised above their backs in display. This contrasts with their white primary feathers, enhancing their striking appearance.

Black Swans occur throughout Australia, but they breed mostly in the south of the continent, in western Australia, South Australia, southern New South Wales, and Victoria, as well as in Tasmania. A few also breed in central Queensland and northern New South Wales. The total population is thought to number between 300,000 and 500,000. In the late nineteenth century, 30 swans were introduced into New Zealand, and within 100 years the population had expanded to over 100,000 individuals. Although it was thought that some of this massive increase might be due to simultaneous immigration from Australia, this seems unlikely as Black Swans had never been recorded in New Zealand before. This population has declined in recent years and probably now numbers no more than 40,000.

Black Swans have been introduced into Europe in small numbers but have never become established in the wild. They probably suffer from competition with other swans and also from predation, both of which were absent in New Zealand when the first Black Swans were released there.

Whistling (or Tundra) Swans

Whistling (or Tundra) Swans from North America are distinguished by their black bills which usually have a tiny teardrop of yellow in the corner by the eye. Their compatriot,

Europeans refused to believe in the existence of a Black Swan when reports
of its discovery first came to them in the seventeenth century.

the Trumpeter Swan, also, confusingly, has a black bill but without the yellow teardrop. However, Whistling Swans are considerably smaller, weighing on average 6.7kg (14.8lb), compared to the Trumpeter's 10.7kg (23.6lb), with relatively shorter necks and shorter, more rounded bodies. Their call is higher-pitched and sounds more like a bugle than a trumpet. Whistling Swans are also much more numerous and widely distributed. In summer they breed on the arctic tundra in Alaska and Canada, and in winter they are found on wetlands near the Atlantic and Pacific coasts of the USA. Those wintering in the eastern United States now number around 110,000 individuals, while those wintering in the west number around 60,000.

Whistling Swans make the longest migrations of all swans. Individuals journeying from breeding grounds in Alaska to wintering grounds along the Pacific seaboard may fly 4,500km (2,796 miles). Those flying south-east from Alaska and arctic Canada to the eastern seaboard of the USA may fly up to 6,000km (3,728 miles). Some swans breed as far east as Southampton Island, but the highest densities are found at the western end of the range in Alaska, where they breed on coastal tundra in the north, west and south-west of the State. A few Whistling Swans have been recorded breeding regularly on the Chukotka Peninsula across the Bering Straits in Russia, and these birds, including several mixed Whistling Swan / Bewick's Swan pairs, have been recorded wintering both on the Pacific seaboard of the USA and also in Japan. You might expect that all the Whistling Swans breeding in Alaska would head south to the nearest wintering grounds in western Canada and USA, but this is not so. Recent research on marked birds shows that the dividing line between those birds heading east to the Atlantic seaboard and those heading south lies in north-west Alaska, between Point Hope and Wainwright. Only those birds breeding south of Point Hope head down the Pacific coast. This surprisingly lengthy migration of the eastern population may be a consequence of a split in the breeding range during the last Ice Age. After the glaciation, the birds in the eastern population spread north-west in search of nesting habitat faster

Whistling Swans typically have a teardrop of yellow on the bill.

western birds spread east. The high density of breeding swans in Alaska suggests that this is indeed the most productive habitat.

In the winter, Whistling Swans prefer areas of open water and marsh, but, with legs set forward on the body, they are also well adapted for walking on land. This has made it easier for them to exploit new food sources such as waste corn and root crops in recent times, when mechanisation has resulted in less efficient harvesting of crops for human consumption. As with the other swans, males are slightly larger than females (weighing 15% more on average), but otherwise the sexes are similar in appearance.

Bewick's Swans

Bewick's Swans are the smallest of the northern swans, weighing around 6kg (13.2lb). They too are among the great travellers. Each spring they migrate from their wintering grounds in temperate Europe and Asia to breeding grounds on the arctic tundra in Russia – 4,000km (2,485 miles) away. Each autumn they return when the arctic begins to freeze. The western population, currently numbering about 18,000 individuals, winters in Denmark, Germany, Holland, UK and Ireland, and breeds on the tundra in European Russia. A few, perhaps up to 600, may head south to the Caspian Sea. The eastern population, breeding on the tundra in Asian Russia, mostly winters in Japan, China and Korea. The population size of eastern Bewick's Swans is not well known, but probably numbers around 30,000. These eastern birds used to be classified as a separate race, known as Jankowski's swan. Though they may be slightly larger and tend to have less yellow on the bill, perhaps because of interbreeding with Whistling Swans across the Bering Straits, they are not different in other respects.

Bewick's Swans usually prefer open habitats including large lakes, marshes and flooded pasture, and are not often found on small water courses. As a result of this and their natural wariness, people have seldom been able to get close to them. So it was not until 1830 that Bewick's Swans were distinguished from the other Eurasian migratory swan, the Whooper Swan. This is perhaps unsurprising since, apart from a difference in size, the distinguishing features are all on the head, which must be seen

Bewick's Swans have more yellow on the bill than Whistling Swans but the yellow stops short of the nostril.

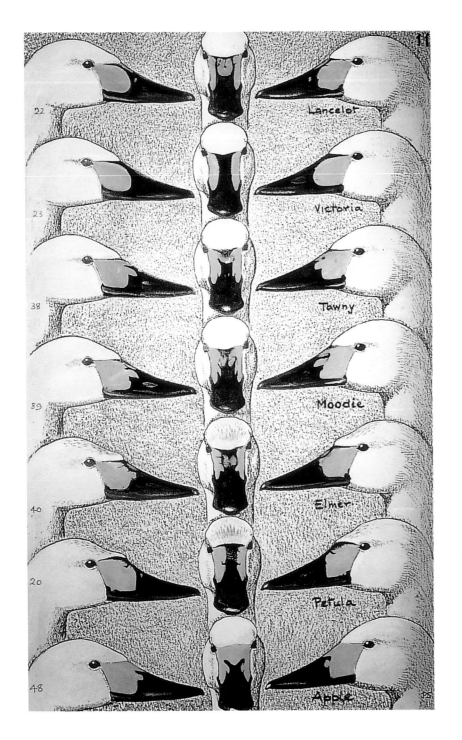

Bill Patterns of Bewick's Swans

Like fingerprints, the pattern of black and yellow on the bills of Bewick's Swans differs between individuals. Scientists at the Wildfowl & Wetlands Trust have used this to recognise and study individuals since February 1964, when my father, Peter Scott, first observed the differences. He found that the patterns differed in many ways, and he drew all the birds that came to the pond in front of his house. In the autumn of 1964, when the swans returned for the winter, he was delighted to recognise the same individuals he had recorded the previous winter. Here again were Lancelot and Victoria, Pink and Rebecca and several other faithful pairs.

Since then Lancelot has become famous at Slimbridge as one of the oldest known wild Bewick's Swans. Already an adult in 1963-4, he returned each winter for a further 22 years. His mate, Victoria, sadly died in 1969. Later, he took another mate, Elaine, with whom he raised two cygnets.

clearly for identification. Bewick's Swans have a small yellow patch on each side of the bill, which does not extend as far as the nostril. Whooper Swans have a larger, wedge-shaped patch of yellow, which extends beneath the nostril along the side of the bill. This difference was first documented by an eighteenth-century English ornithologist, William Yarrell, who named the smaller swan in honour of the famous naturalist and wood-engraver, Thomas Bewick.

The movements of Bewick's Swans in winter have altered somewhat during the twentieth century as a result of changing conditions. During the 1950s increasing numbers of Bewick's Swans were seen in the Netherlands, where they were finding food in the enclosed Ijsselmeer. But in the 1960s the water plants that had supported them in the Netherlands began to disappear and the swans came further west. Small numbers were visiting the estuary of the river Severn at Slimbridge where my father, Peter Scott, had established the Wildfowl Trust (now Wildfowl & Wetlands Trust), an organisation dedicated to the conservation and study of wildfowl and their habitats.

Drawn down by the calls of Whistling Swans in the collection at Slimbridge, the first wild Bewick's Swans flew in to the pond in front of my father's house. As he watched from his studio window, he noticed that the pattern of black and yellow on the bill was different on each bird, and he was able to recognise individuals within the flock. He began to draw the faces of the different swans as they came, and gave them names so that he could remember them. He soon found that he could identify all 24 of the individuals that came in that winter of 1963-4. In the following years the numbers of Bewick's Swans visiting Slimbridge grew to several hundred, and the study of individuals also grew. It became clear that, like goose flocks, Bewick's Swan flocks are composed of pairs, families and single individuals and that the same swans would return to Slimbridge year after year. Since then the histories of several thousand swans have been followed. Their successes and failures in attracting mates and rearing young have been documented, as well as the details of their behaviour. For example, some pairs make good parents, keeping their cygnets close to them constantly, while some regularly manage to lose their young.

Like Whistling, Whooper and Trumpeter Swans, Bewick's Swans are very vocal, making contact calls frequently and bugling loudly when involved in aggressive display. Again, males and females are similar in appearance, but males are slightly larger (13% heavier) and have slightly heavier bills.

Whooper Swans

Whooper Swans are substantially larger than Bewick's Swans, weighing 9.8kg (21.6lb), but like them have a yellow and black bill. Apart from the difference in body size, the best way to distinguish Whoopers from Bewick's Swans is by the length of the yellow patch on the side of the bill, which extends to a point beneath the nostril in Whoopers but stops short, in a rounded or square patch, on Bewick's Swans. In contrast to the musical bugling of Bewick's, Whooper Swan calls sound jangling and strident, especially in display. They too are very vocal, making softer calls frequently to maintain contact with other individuals. Birds also call loudly when they become separated from mate or family, for example when they land at opposite ends of a lake, or are scattered among other flock members.

Whooper Swans are Eurasian, breeding across the arctic, mostly in the taiga zone where lakes are set among stands of conifers and birches. Their range extends from Iceland in the west to the far north-east of Russia. The majority of birds breeding in Iceland come south to winter in the UK and Ireland; this population numbers about 18,000, of which up to 1,000 stay through the winter in southern Iceland on waters warmed by hot springs. Whoopers breeding in Scandinavia and European Russia probably winter in western Europe – in Sweden, Denmark and Germany. Further east, those breeding in the central Russian taiga probably winter mainly on the Black and Caspian seas, and those breeding in eastern Siberia winter mainly in Japan, China and Korea. A very few have been recorded across the Bering Straits in Alaska and a few have wintered in the Aleutian Islands.

The size of the continental populations is not clear, though the total is probably less than 100,000. Little is known of the migratory movements of Russian Whoopers, or

In Whooper Swans the wedge of yellow on the bill extends below the nostril.

*Whooper Swans breeding in north-eastern Russia spend the winter
in Japan, where they are found on lakes and sea coasts.*

how much interchange there is between the different wintering populations. A few of the birds that winter in Denmark have also been observed in Britain, and some of the Icelandic Whoopers, from the eastern part of the island, regularly winter on mainland Europe, suggesting some interchange between the Icelandic and continental breeding populations.

Whooper Swans are the most aggressive of the Eurasian swans, and dominate both Mutes and Bewick's when they meet in winter flocks. Normally the wintering range of Whooper Swans tends to be further north than that of Bewick's Swans, though recently Whoopers have expanded their range south from Scotland into England, coming into contact with Bewick's Swans both in Lancashire and on the Ouse Washes in Cambridgeshire. Similarly, in America, Trumpeter Swans, which are large, tend to winter further north than the smaller Whistling (Tundra) Swan. This is probably because they can survive colder conditions better, having a smaller surface area : volume ratio. This trend, known as Bergmann's rule, is found in many groups of animals.

By contrast, in the summer we see the reverse. In Eurasia Whooper Swans breed south of Bewick's Swans, and in America Trumpeter Swans tend to breed south of Whistling (Tundra) swans. It seems likely that this is because the smaller species, which grow faster, can rear their young in the shorter tundra summer, while the larger species need the longer taiga season to rear their young.

Trumpeter Swans

Trumpeter Swans are the largest of all the species, weighing on average 10.7kg (23.6lb), with a wingspan of 2.97m (10ft). These magnificent birds were once widespread in North America but were very nearly hunted to extinction. Throughout the nineteenth century, thousands were killed for their down and feathers. By 1932 it was estimated that only 69 individuals existed, though this did not include a few thousand individuals in Alaska which were not hunted to the same extent. Now, following strict protection measures, the southern population numbers up to 2,800 and the Alaskan population around 13,300 individuals.

The southern population once bred from central Canada east to Hudson Bay, and wintered as far south as the Gulf of Mexico. The remaining birds are now confined to two small localised populations, one sedentary in the Rocky Mountains in Idaho, Wyoming and Montana, known as the 'tristate' population, numbering about 600, and the other in interior Canada, in British Columbia and Alberta, numbering about 2,200. Together these two small groups are known as the Rocky Mountain population. The 'tristate' population is descended from sedentary trumpeters which escaped hunting by remaining in remote places throughout the year , for example on water bodies warmed by hot springs. Even today these swans are more or less sedentary. Because each locality can only support a limited number of swans, efforts are being made to re-establish populations in other areas, so as to increase this small population above its current level. In contrast, the interior Canadian and Alaskan populations are still migratory, the former joining the 'tristate' population in winter and the latter moving from breeding grounds in the taiga habitat towards the interior of the state, south, to winter along the Pacific coast in British Columbia.

Although Trumpeter Swans are now completely protected, hunters do occasionally shoot them claiming they mistook them for Whistling (Tundra) Swans, which are legal quarry in some areas. Sometimes it can be difficult to distinguish the two species visually at long range but the best cue is the voice. The Trumpeter's call is more strident, the Whistling Swan's more bugling and clear. Trumpeter Swans are also considerably bigger, longer in proportion, and as adults their bills are always completely black. Again, males are slightly larger than females (25% heavier) and have deeper bills, but otherwise they are similar in appearance.

Parent swans, like this Trumpeter, often stir up small food items for their cygnets by 'trampling' or 'treadling' with their feet.

*Non-breeding Whooper Swans feed on submerged
vegetation in Lake Myvatn, Iceland, in summer.*

Feeding and Migrating

Swans are the giraffes of the bird world. Their long necks enable them to reach below the surface to depths between 50 and 110cm (20-43in) to feed on underwater vegetation. If they cannot reach just by lowering the neck, then the whole body tips up and the swan may remain up-ended for over a minute. The serrations on their bills and tongues help them to grip the vegetation, and also to sieve out particles from the water. Sometimes swans will paddle on the spot in order to clear mud from the roots of aquatic plants or to break up the plant stems. Parents may stir up small items for their cygnets by 'trampling' or 'treadling' in this way.

Most adult swans are entirely vegetarian, though there are some exceptions. Whistling (Tundra) Swans in Chesapeake Bay have discovered that shellfish are good to eat, and about 30% of their diet at the Eastern Neck Wildlife Refuge is composed of clams (*Macoma baltica* and *Mya arenaria*). Mute Swans may inadvertently consume substantial numbers of invertebrates which live on water plants. But, contrary to popular claims, they do not eat fish. The only time when swans regularly take animal food is during the first two weeks of life, when cygnets of the northern swans eat insect larvae.

The diet of swans varies with the quality and availability of different items. In the autumn, winter and early spring, when stems and leaves have withered or contain little nourishment, the swans will dig down for roots, tubers and stolons of plants such as sago pondweed. These are also the first foods available for migratory swans arriving on their breeding grounds in the spring. Later, as the vegetation grows, the swans eat a variety of emerging grasses, sedges and other plants.

Human impact on north temperate wetlands in the twentieth century has meant that there are much fewer areas where swans can feed undisturbed on aquatic plants and this may have contributed to a decline in numbers and breeding success in some areas, especially in the 1960s. However, the northern swans have discovered other sources of food. With increased use of fertiliser, low-lying pastures have become more nutritious, and swans now visit riverine pastures to graze, especially in spring. Modern hi-tech harvesting methods mean that gleanings of grain, small potatoes, sugar beet, and turnip tops are left lying on the land, and once frosted and soft, these are good food for swans. Vast hedgeless fields make a safe habitat where predators can be seen before they pose a danger.

Taking waste crops seldom upsets farmers, but grazing winter wheat can pose problems. Usually grazing encourages grass and wheat to 'tiller', or grow new side-shoots, which increases the density of the eventual crop. In this respect farmers do not worry unduly if the grazing is light. Damage is most likely when the ground is wet and the swans' large feet trample and squash down the shoots in sticky earth. Then it becomes necessary for farmers to scare the swans away from their land.

Estimating the daily food requirements of swans is difficult, but studies of Bewick's Swans feeding on sago pondweed tubers indicate that one swan consumes about 280gm (9.9oz) (dry weight) per day. But food intake varies considerably depending on the time of year and food availability. Before and during the breeding season food requirements increase. Females eat more before egg-laying and incubation, and both sexes lay down fat reserves before migration.

The risks associated with migration are great. Food supplies may have failed at a traditional site and alternatives may not be available nearby. Weather conditions may force a retreat or blow the swans off course. Predators may have increased unexpectedly at a well known haunt. The journey itself is energetically demanding. This is particularly apparent for Whooper Swans breeding in Iceland, since they cross at least 800km (497 miles) of sea with no possibility of re-fuelling on the way. An exciting new study of Whooper Swans used satellite tracking to follow two breeding females from Iceland to their wintering place at Caerlaverock on the Solway Firth in Scotland. Previous studies have indicated that swans sometimes migrate at high altitudes, even as high as 8,000m (26,247ft), but these two, after climbing initially, then came down towards sea-level and cruised low. Unexpectedly too, they both stopped for a rest on the sea. Two different individuals were tracked back to Iceland the following spring,

*Whistling (or Tundra) Swans make the longest
migrations of all the swans. Individuals may fly 6,000km
(3,728 miles) from breeding grounds in northern Alaska to wintering
grounds in eastern USA, stopping at traditional sites along
the way. The risks involved are considerable.*

Migration is clearly exhausting. When Bewick's
Swans arrive at Slimbridge in autumn, they often sleep for
much of the first day. Here they are asleep or resting on the ice on
Matsalu Bay, in Estonia, a traditional stopover site on the
way to their breeding grounds in arctic Russia.

again indicating the difficulties of migrating. Both individuals encountered strong contrary winds over the sea, which blew them off course. Just when they seemed about to miss Iceland altogether, they altered direction appropriately, and came in safely, but the journey had taken five days for one of them, 29 hours for the other.

Scientists who have flown micro-light aircraft with migrating Whistling (Tundra) Swans discovered that they too fly long distances between staging posts, in some instances up to 700km (430 miles). To minimise the costs of migration, swans usually wait until the weather is favourable before beginning a journey. So they tend to set off in clear weather, not cloud, with a tail wind and not into a head wind.

The lengthy migrations undertaken by the northern swans seem costly and dangerous. The precise costs are not easy to measure, but the energetic costs are evident in the low weights of Bewick's Swans arriving on the wintering grounds after the autumn migration. So why do the swans make such long migrations? The benefits must be substantial to offset these costs. It seems likely that one of the principal benefits lies in the extended day length at high latitudes, which has two consequences for the swans. First, the swans can feed 24 hours a day. Normally swans seldom feed in the dark, especially if they are relying on land-based food, such as grasses or waste crops. Second and most important, the vegetation grows faster and shows a massive increase in productivity at the time when the swans need good food for breeding. Cygnets usually hatch as the period of greatest productivity is beginning and benefit from it by achieving maximum growth rates. For example, Whooper Swan cygnets hatching at subarctic and arctic latitudes in the wild fledge in around 9-10 weeks, while cygnets of Mute Swans breeding at low latitudes usually take 14 or more weeks to fledge.

While the search for quality food leads the swans on long journeys, the local distribution of their food affects their dispersal and social behaviour. During the non-breeding season, most swans congregate in areas of high food availability, forming flocks of varying size. Flocks also provide safety in numbers. During migration swans will stop at traditional staging areas, many of which are large areas of open shallow water or large pastures where there is enough food for large if transitory flocks to build up.

Disputes between pairs and families may escalate, involving spectacular wing-waving displays and simultaneous calling.

However, within flocks of swans there is considerable competition for food, and as in many animals, large dominant individuals are more successful than smaller ones at winning arguments and gaining access to the best food. If you watch a flock of swans feeding on waste crops or on aquatic vegetation for some time, you will notice frequent threats or displays by some swans directed at others, with the dominant bird or pair eventually displacing the other. Sometimes these threats are not contested and losers move away quickly. At other times a dispute ensues which may escalate. Opponents then display vigorously at each other. Mute Swans, Black Swans and Black-necked Swans raise their wings and may lunge at opponents. The four northern migratory swans engage in a series of spectacular wing-waving displays while calling loudly. Partners of pairs display together in a concerted effort to intimidate opponents. As among geese, such arguments are usually won by pairs with cygnets over those without, and pairs with more cygnets tend to defeat those with fewer, though this is not always so. Similarly, pairs usually dominate single birds. Because small birds are less successful than large birds, single females are especially vulnerable, as are orphaned cygnets or those separated from their parents.

This helps to explain why cygnets usually stay with their parents beyond fledging, unlike ducklings which part company from their parents as soon as they can fly. Ducklings reach adult size by their first autumn, but cygnets are only around three-quarters adult size by their first autumn. Cygnets separated from their parents are continually threatened and chased in flocks and spend little time feeding. Parents, because they are dominant, are able to protect their young. Family ties are especially strong in the migratory swans.

During the breeding season, most swans are highly territorial. For a breeding pair to ensure an adequate food supply for themselves during nesting and for their brood, they will defend an area which in the northern migratory swans may be as large as a square kilometre (one-half square mile). Defence is fierce and impressive, involving spectacular displays. If all else fails, opponents will resort to physical combat, the males grabbing each other by the base of the neck and beating each other with their wings.

The boundaries of the territory may change slightly as the cygnets grow, but the family usually stays in the area until they fledge.

Young birds and some breeding birds that fail to gain territories may spend part of the summer in flocks feeding on lakes, rivers or estuaries, and families with cygnets may join these flocks before migrating.

Although most swans are territorial in the breeding season and will not tolerate other swans nesting nearby, there are exceptions. In contrast to the white swans, Black Swans are not territorial and breed in colonies on large lakes, where neighbouring nests may be as little as one metre (3.3ft) apart. The breeding season for Black Swans usually coincides with fluctuating water levels so that new food sources are constantly being exposed. Consequently, there is usually enough food within range of the colony to support its inhabitants.

Among the northern swans, only Mute Swans ever breed in colonies, and these occur on large lakes or in coastal areas where the swans have access to large areas of aquatic vegetation. As with Black Swans, colonies are a spectacular sight, with nesting birds less than 2m (6.6ft) apart and swans continually grunting and displaying at each other. Colonies occur in Denmark, Sweden, western Germany, Russia and the UK. However, detailed studies of colonial Mute Swans at Abbotsbury, UK and at Roskildefjord in Denmark, suggest that pairs in colonies breed less successfully than pairs defending territories. Birds in colonies hatch fewer eggs and rear fewer cygnets to fledging. This is probably because pairs interfere with each other and because food supplies do sometimes become depleted around large colonies.

Non-breeding Whooper Swans feed on a fjord in eastern Iceland.

Surviving and Breeding

Being the size of a swan has a number of consequences. Large animals tend to have slower growth rates, slower breeding rates and longer lives. All the swans fit this description, as do geese, especially in comparison with their smaller relatives the ducks.

On average swans take two years to reach adult size, and they lay fewer eggs each year than ducks. The average clutch size among swans is about five eggs, while an average dabbling duck lays about nine eggs per clutch and may lay more than one clutch each year. Swans have been known to live for more than 30 years in captivity, and they are also long-lived in the wild. At the Wildfowl & Wetlands Trust at Slimbridge, the oldest known wild Bewick's Swan, called Casino, was still visiting Swan Lake in 1994-5 at the age of 26, having first arrived as a cygnet with her parents in 1968. In comparison, ducks seldom survive beyond ten years.

Slow growth rates are a problem, though, for the northern migratory swans that breed at high latitudes. The young must be fledged before the onset of the arctic autumn or they will die. Over the course of their history this has meant strong natural selection for individuals with faster growth rates, and as a result, these four swans have higher growth rates as cygnets than have the other swans, size for size. The inclusion of insects in the cygnets' diet may help to speed up their growth. These cygnets also fledge relatively sooner. They can fly when they are still only 75% as heavy as their parents. But this means that by the time they reach the wintering grounds they are still substantially smaller than their parents and so benefit considerably from parental protection.

Slow growth rates mean late maturation and age at first breeding. In ideal conditions swans may be physically capable of breeding at the age of two. In captivity female Black Swans have been recorded laying eggs at one year old and males may become physically mature by 20 months. But in the wild, breeding so early is very seldom possible. First a swan must find a suitable partner and then it must find, and

Whooper Swan cygnets must grow quickly in the short northern summer.

often compete for, a nesting site or territory. In practise most swans pair at two or three years old and attempt to nest soon after. Observations of known individuals whose histories have been followed since their first winter show that, while the less migratory swans (Black, Black-necked and Mute Swans) usually manage to breed successfully around age four, the more migratory swans (Trumpeter, Whooper, Whistling and Bewick's Swans) do not normally raise young until they are over five years old. In Europe, Bewick's Swans do not usually raise young successfully until they are seven years old, while Icelandic Whooper Swans can succeed at the age of five. This is probably a consequence of the greater difficulties associated with longer migrations and high arctic breeding, so that only after they have gained some experience do birds become successful.

Now that individual swans have been studied over long periods, we know that Bewick's and Whooper Swans, up to the age of 12 years, become increasingly successful in raising young.

This might seem surprising but consider the energetic costs and the risks involved in breeding. All swans build large nests 3-4m (10-13ft) across near water, often on islands or promontories. At the same time they must defend their territory against intruders. For the northern migratory swans there is the additional problem that the breeding grounds are often still under snow when the birds arrive and the swans must then decide whether to retreat to the last suitable feeding place and risk losing their territory to another pair, or sit it out till the snow melts. Frequently, they choose the latter, and early spring on the tundra may find camouflaged pairs of swans sleeping on the snow, waking only to advertise their occupation with aggressive bugling calls when potential rivals appear. As the snow and ice melt, feeding areas become accessible and the birds can begin to recoup energy used up on migration. Observations have shown that apart from building or repairing the nest and defending the territory, pairs spend much of their time feeding. The female then lays her eggs, usually one every other day, and begins to incubate them when the clutch is complete. If the spring is late the clutch will be smaller, partly because the female's reserves, built up before and during

The costs of breeding are high. Territorial
fights like this one between two Mute Swan cobs can result in
injury. The males usually grab each other at the base of the neck and
beat each other with their wings. However, losing a territory
means losing the chance to breed at all in that year.

migration, will have been reduced while waiting. The swans are also geared to laying fewer eggs later because, if incubation is delayed, fledging will also be delayed beyond the beginning of autumn and the cygnets may not survive. In addition, the cygnets would then hatch after the period of highest food productivity. Not surprisingly, the northern migratory swans tend to lay smaller clutches (4.4 eggs on average) than the less migratory swans (5.6 eggs).

Recent studies of Bewick's Swans breeding in arctic Russia have highlighted the problems facing the swans. Territories are fiercely contested, the weather is unpredictable and temperatures often plummet below zero even after an initial thaw. Evidence is beginning to accumulate that partners must act as a team, and that the longer they have been together, the more successful they become. Among Bewick's Swans, the breeding success of pairs increases rapidly during the first few years they are together, and continues to increase slowly even after that. Whooper Swan pairs also become more successful with time, at least for the first six years. If a swan loses its partner it must begin again with a new mate. In addition, the migratory swans usually take more than one year to find a new mate and breed again.

This helps to explain why 'divorce' is so uncommon in swans. Fewer than 6% of Whooper Swans and 4% of Mute Swans change partner while their first partner is alive. No case of 'divorce' has been recorded among Bewick's Swans that have bred successfully together. In over 2,500 pairs, only one case has ever been observed. This involved a pair at Welney in Norfolk, UK, which separated after seven years together, during which time they had never raised young. The female, named Olive, returned one year with a new partner and cygnets, and went on to breed in two of the three years that she subsequently returned with him. The original male returned for two years after the separation but did not take another mate. In this particular instance changing partner appeared to benefit the female. Usually however, changing mates reduces a swan's breeding success for a time, and as such is likely to be disadvantageous in the long run. Exactly how the teamwork operates within pairs is not yet clear.

In most swan species only the female incubates, though the male may sit on the

During incubation swans stand up and turn their eggs at regular intervals.

nest when the female goes off to feed. If the nest is left unattended, the eggs are usually covered with nest material to hide them from predators. In Whistling, Bewick's and Black Swans, however, both sexes incubate, and unless both sexes have to defend the territory together, this means that the nest is less likely to be unattended. Male Whistling and Bewick's Swans will sit for about one third of the time and females for two thirds. In Black Swans, males take a slightly greater share in incubation than females and their contribution increases during the incubation period. Incubation lasts between 30 and 36 days. The four high-latitude breeders all have shorter incubation periods than the others, with Bewick's Swans having the shortest at 30 days and Black Swans the longest at 36 days.

During this long period, incubating birds are vulnerable to predators, and the benefits of being large are clear. Swans (unlike ducks) are able to defend their nests against most predators including eagles and foxes as well as egg thieves such as gulls and skuas (jaegers). In the arctic, threatened swans display and call, and their mates usually fly to join them in a spectacular defence involving feather-bristling, wing-flapping and bugling. The only serious threat to adults is man. In many areas of the arctic, indigenous peoples have long harvested swans on a regular basis. This means that Whistling and Bewick's Swans especially are very wary of people. Because of their acute eyesight, they see people well before people can see them and their first reaction is to hide, flattening themselves on the nest with their necks laid out, snake-like, across the nest wall. Then if the danger increases, they will creep off, heads low, and steal down to the nearest water to swim away.

Because incubation does not generally begin until the clutch is complete, all the eggs usually hatch within 24 hours. Downy cygnets are particularly vulnerable during the first two weeks of life. In the arctic the greatest risks are predators such as arctic foxes and snowy owls, as well as bad weather and consequent lack of food. For the first few weeks, the female broods the young under her wings during rain. Northern swans

Cygnets are at their most vulnerable in the first two weeks of life.

always brood their cygnets on land, but the temperate swans (Mute, Black-necked and Black Swans) will carry their cygnets on their backs in the water, brooding them under and between their folded wings.

As the cygnets grow, their vulnerability to predators decreases, though people and foxes remain serious hazards. Surprisingly, foxes will occasionally take adult swans unaware and kill them. A warden at the Wildfowl & Wetlands Trust reserve at Welney in Norfolk, UK, watched a fox grab an adult Whooper Swan at the base of the neck and hold on, despite a struggle, until the bird suffocated. However this was probably an exceptionally brave or hungry fox. In most cases an adult swan's hissing threat will deter a fox.

Studies of Whistling Swans have shown that migration results in many casualties for newly-fledged cygnets making their first journey. Just over half the cygnets recorded in mid-August survive until mid-December. Many of those that fail to survive are shot by hunters. In the United States, Whistling Swans are legal quarry in some areas. By contrast, in Europe, all swan species are protected. However, they are still shot regularly. By taking X-rays of individual swans when they are caught, scientists from WWT in UK have found that 30-40% of adult Bewick's Swans carry lead shot in their tissues. One individual, named Pie, carried 21 pellets.

Other causes of mortality among swans include flying accidents, lead poisoning and disease. Because swans are heavily wing-loaded, with a relatively small wing area for their body weight, they cannot easily fly slowly. Rapid manoeuvres are therefore difficult and avoiding obstacles at short notice can be a serious problem. These conditions occur both when it is foggy and when it is very windy. Swans regularly collide with overhead cables in fog, and sometimes crash-land around trees. Alternatively they may see the cables at the last minute and stop flying, which may prove equally fatal. I once watched a Mute Swan do this. Luckily it landed on soft ground and walked away without trouble. But many swans die of internal damage caused on impact with the ground.

Lead poisoning as a result of ingesting spent lead shot or anglers' discarded fishing weights is another major cause of mortality. In UK 20% of all adult swans found dead

After their downy plumage, cygnets develop grey or grey-brown plumage.
Only after about a year do they become white.

Despite their significance in myths and legends, swans have been hunted and exploited.

had succumbed to lead poisoning. Because the swans need grit in their gizzards to grind up their food, they selectively swallow tiny stones. Unfortunately lead pellets are an appropriate size. As the pellets are ground down in the gizzard, they form soluble lead salts which are absorbed into the bloodstream, causing a slow and painful death. It may take as few as two or three pellets to kill a swan. Each time a gun is fired, 250 pellets are scattered over a wide area where they will remain indefinitely. Only a few are needed to kill the target. As a result, many areas of marshland are covered with lead shot.

A Bewick's Swan prospects for a nest.

Anglers' pellets are frequently lost or discarded on the banks of rivers and lakes after use. Those that fall in the water are within the normal feeding range of Mute Swans. In the late 1970s, Mute Swans began to suffer from lead poisoning in increasing numbers. Large flocks in towns and cities dwindled, including the well-known flock at Stratford-upon-Avon in Warwickshire, UK. Initially the cause was not clear. Why should so many swans suddenly suffer from lead poisoning? It was not as if there had been a sudden increase in the popularity of angling. However, detailed research showed that lead poisoning was indeed the cause of the increased swan mortality, and suggested that the lead in the environment had reached a critical level where swans were likely to encounter pellets frequently when feeding. As a result, in 1987, the UK government introduced a ban on the sale, import and use of lead angling weights between 0.06g (0.002oz) and 28.36g (1oz) (no. 8 split shot, 1oz leger). This has resulted in less frequent deaths from this cause and to a return of the urban flocks. So far a voluntary ban on the use of lead for shooting has been agreed, but not a statutory ban. Hopefully lead will soon be replaced by a satisfactory alternative shot.

Among wild swans, disease is a regular, though less obvious cause of mortality. Juvenile swans appear to be more susceptible to disease than adults. Young Mute Swans have been found suffering from infection by a parasitic nematode (*Acuaria uncinata*) while juvenile Whooper and Bewick's Swans suffer from aspergillosis, an infection by the fungus *Aspergillus fumigatus* which attacks the lungs. Among wintering Whistling Swans of the western population, avian cholera, a bacterial infection by *Pasteurella multocida*, causes sporadic but sometimes substantial mortality. In January and February 1975, 1,004 Whistling Swans died from cholera in California. A similar epidemic occurred there again in the winter of 1987-8. Swans are also sometimes parasitized by heartworms *Sarconema enryurea*, which may cause serious damage to the heart muscles. As with many diseases there is a close relationship between the condition of the animal and the ability of the parasite to survive and multiply in its host. Swans in poor condition are more likely to suffer heavy infestations of parasites and to succumb to disease.

One bacterium that can kill swans, though without causing disease, is *Clostridium botulinum* which produces a lethal toxin. This bacterium can become common in the anaerobic conditions found in warm shallow alkaline waters where waterfowl come to feed, and may cause many sudden deaths. Outbreaks of botulism among swans have been recorded in Europe, America and Australia.

Another poison hazardous to swans is oil. Small-scale pollution with oil is widespread and large spillages have caused the deaths of hundreds of swans, especially Mute Swans which congregate in docks and estuaries. So far, no mass mortality has occurred among the migratory swans, though oil exploration and leaking pipelines in the arctic represent an increasing hazard, particularly for the least common of the swans: Bewick's Swan.

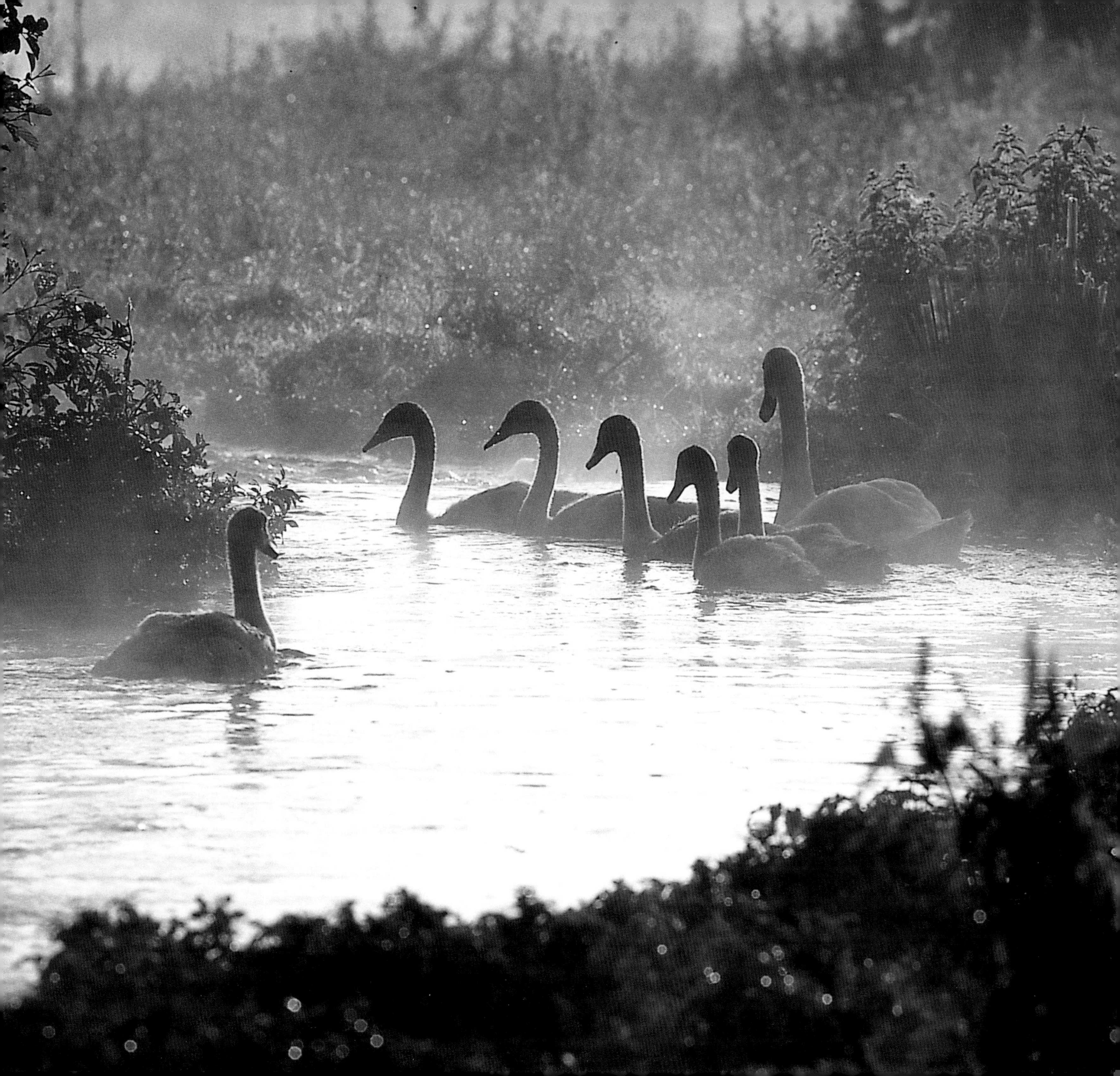

Exploitation

The first indication of the importance of swans to people is in drawings of swan-like birds dating from the Stone Age. Later, tethered Mute Swans are depicted in delicate applique on the shroud of a Scythian chieftain who died in Pazyrak in central Siberia around 500 BC. Subsequent artistic representations of swans show their importance in myths and legends, as well as celebrating their beauty.

Despite their mythical significance, swans have been hunted and exploited in different ways by humans throughout prehistory and history, as the chieftain's shroud demonstrates. It seems likely that low-density human populations have often exploited swans when possible. On the breeding grounds, eggs and young have been taken, and adults too, when they become flightless. Because non-breeding birds tend to move to large areas of water, large flocks may develop. To primitive peoples these flocks represented a valuable supply of food. In the North American arctic, flightless Tundra Swans were hunted by Eskimos using kayaks to force the birds onto land where they could be chased and speared more easily. In Iceland, hunters would ride down Whooper Swans on horseback, and send forward dogs to hold the swans down until the rider arrived.

As human populations increased and greater food supplies were needed, techniques became more ambitious. In Russia, hunters used sailing boats to drive the swans into nets where they would catch several hundred Whooper Swans in a day. Records also indicate that large numbers of Whooper Swans were caught in this way on the wintering grounds in Iran, an operation which would have required some skill to ensure that the swans did not take flight to avoid being caught.

Since the invention of firearms swans have been at risk throughout the year, and this has increased the opportunities for exploitation. From the late eighteenth century swans were hunted for their skins. Their flight feathers were also taken for use as quill pens. The Hudson's Bay Company sold hundreds of thousands of swan skins from North America on the London market between about 1770 and 1900, until there were so few swans left that the trade ceased. This trade decimated the continental North American population of Trumpeter Swans and it was estimated that a mere 69 individuals remained alive in 1933. Luckily the Alaskan population had not suffered so badly. Even so, the species was now very rare.

Black-necked and Bewick's Swans also suffered from the trade in pelts during the nineteenth century. One American observer recorded hundreds of thousands of Black-necked Swan skins awaiting shipment in an Argentinian warehouse. Swan skins were highly valued because of their toughness and the great thickness of white down which made boas and other items for women, as well as wallets, jackets and caps. Bewick's Swans were still being hunted commercially in the USSR until the 1930s, when swans became protected throughout the country. A fashionable item for women in the north was a swan-feather hat. Now with political instability and poverty in Russia, the swans may again be at risk.

A Mute Swan in flight.

Legalised hunting of Whistling Swans occurs in a number of states in the USA. The total bag is around 3,000 swans from the eastern population and 1,200 from the western population, although about 10,000 permits are issued annually. As both populations have expanded since the special swan hunting seasons were established in 1962, this level of shooting does not appear to threaten the species' survival. Currently none of the other swan species can be hunted legally, except by special permit if they can be shown to be causing damage.

Mute Swans are among the heaviest flying birds. Like aircraft they need long runways to become airborne.

Luckily, Black Swans escaped the great hunt for swan feathers and pelts which decimated the Trumpeter Swan population in North America in the nineteenth century.

Illegal hunting still occurs, however, despite the protection of swans. Some of this is modern subsistence hunting and some is shooting by poachers or vandals, or by farmers whose crops the swans are eating but who have not obtained permits. Subsistence hunters in western Alaska take considerable harvests of waterfowl including swans. One survey of 600 households in the Yukon-Kuskokwim Delta in Alaska indicated that 5,000 or more western-population Whistling Swans were killed each summer, mostly early in the season, and several hundred eggs were also taken. However, the population density of humans in western Alaska is relatively high. Corresponding subsistence hunting pressure in northern Alaska and Canada, where human populations are less dense, is not nearly so heavy.

Although all kinds of swans have been kept in captivity at various times, only one swan has ever been systematically domesticated: the Mute Swan. The practise of swan-keeping was already well established in England by the eleventh century, and also occurred in continental Europe. Swans were caught up as cygnets and kept in swan-pits where they were fattened on malt and barley. They were then ready to eat in October and November when the meat was considered to be tasty but tender. The French named the youngsters 'cygnets', referring only to birds tender enough for the table. In Britain the tradition of swan farming continued until the end of the eighteenth century, while in the Netherlands it went on until the second world war. This method of farming swans did not seriously deplete the breeding population and, to encourage the production of more young, adults were often fed.

One early story gives an impression of the importance attached to flocks of tame swans and also indicates that people were not familiar with the migratory swans at close range. This story tells how in September 1186 on the day of the enthronement of the Bishop of Lincoln, a new kind of swan arrived with 'the bill…becomingly adorned with yellow…,' which then 'slew great numbers of the other royal swans' with 'the knob and black…on the bill.' Finally this aggressive bird (clearly a Whooper Swan) attached itself to the Bishop and fed from his hand. The reference to 'royal' swans indicates that the Crown already claimed ownership of swans. Originally this extended to all swans in the country, but later it included only unmarked swans on the River Thames, a situation which prevails today. Certain important companies and families were given 'royalties' of swans which included the right to own and mark swans and their young.

Owning swans was therefore extremely prestigious, whether they were for ornament or for the table, but it also involved the duty of pinioning and marking the swans. An elaborate system of marks was devised and issued by the Crown to distinguish swans belonging to different owners. Swan rolls were published illustrating these different marks. Swans were usually marked by cutting a pattern of notches into the upper mandible of the bill. This was done in July when the cygnets were half grown, in the annual ceremony of swan-upping. Today, only two city companies, the Worshipful companies of Dyers and Vintners, maintain this tradition. Their appointed swanherds, together with the Queen's Swan Keeper, set out in boats on the River Thames to catch the swans on the river and mark their young, one notch for the Dyers and two for the Vintners.

At Abbotsbury on the Fleet in Dorset, UK, Mute Swans are still managed in the way they were by monks in the eleventh century. Here the swans breed in a colony, nesting on piles of cut reeds which are put out for them at distances of 2-3m (6.5-10ft) apart. Cygnets from the first five nests to hatch are then put with their parents in five small pens. Cygnets from the next nests to hatch are added to these pens until each pen contains 15-20 cygnets with an adult pair. The birds are fed on grain, eel grass, grass clippings and chick-crumbs until mid-September. Nowadays they are then released onto the Fleet, though in past times they would have been taken for the table.

It is perhaps surprising that swans were only domesticated in Eurasia, since all species breed well in captivity today. However, domestication of animals is usually undertaken by sedentary human populations at relatively high density. Since many swan populations frequented areas of low human density in the past, they would have escaped the possibility of domestication.

The Mute Swans at Abbotsbury in Dorset, UK,
were probably domesticated by monks in the eleventh century. Today,
they still breed in a colony and are managed in the traditional way. The cygnets are reared
in pens until mid-September. Nowadays they are then released in the large flock
on the Fleet. In past times they would have been taken for the table.

Swans are protected in most countries. However, with increasing
human populations, swans face new and dangerous hazards.

Conservation

Today, swans are protected in most countries and hunting is restricted. Conservation measures have been successful so far. The story of the Trumpeter Swan illustrates this well. From the original 69 surviving swans in 1933, the 'tristate' population has expanded to 600 swans and is now only limited by the capacity of the environment together with the traditionally sedentary habits of these particular birds. Swans of all kinds are not instinctively migratory. They only migrate if led by their parents, and they tend to rely on traditional sites. To overcome this limit on the population, scientists have recently begun trying to extend the range of these Trumpeter Swans by translocating young birds to other sites. Already some of these birds are returning annually to their new winter quarters.

However, increasing human populations mean that swans run into conflict with farmers more often and face more man-made hazards. Because swans, being large, have a slow rate of reproduction, producing few cygnets per year, they remain vulnerable to increases in mortality and to decreases in breeding success.

Scientists have helped to bring about a ban on the use of lead fishing weights, and are now working towards the phasing out of lead in gunshot, so that fewer swans will suffer a slow death from lead poisoning. They are also monitoring the populations of swans and other species so that changes in numbers become apparent before it is too late to do anything about them. If we remain vigilant in this way, future generations will still be able to watch and enjoy swans. For me there is nothing more exciting than the call of Bewick's Swans, circling downwards from a bright autumn sky, knowing they have flown 4,000km (2,485 miles) from the remote wilderness of the tundra.

World Distribution of Swan Species

Trumpeter Swans

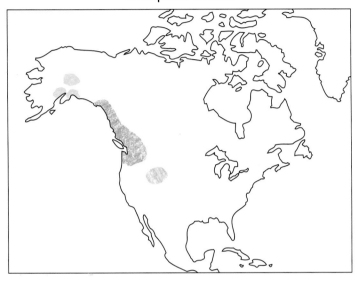

Whistling (or Tundra) Swans

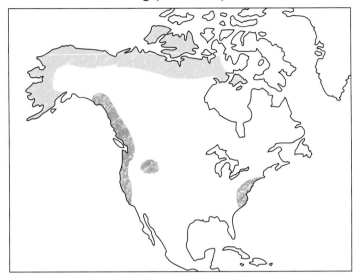

Black-necked Swans

Coscoroba Swans

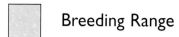 Breeding Range Breeding and Wintering Range Wintering Range

Whooper Swans

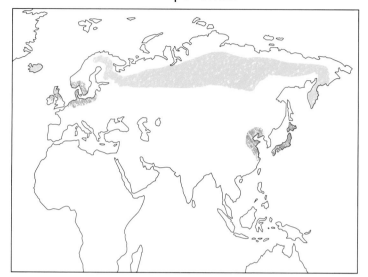

Bewick's Swans

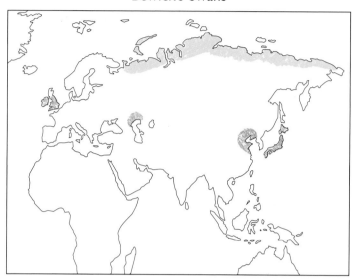

Mute Swans

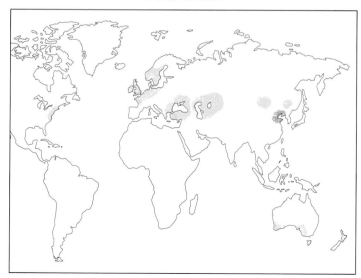

Black Swans

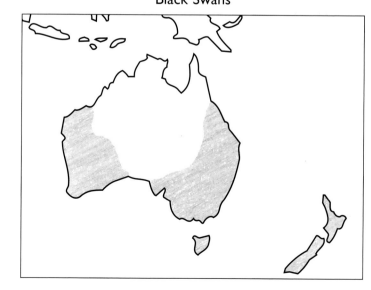

Swan Facts

Scientific Name	Coscoroba Swan	Black-necked Swan	Black Swan	Mute Swan
	Coscoroba coscoroba	*Cygnus melanocoryphus*	*Cygnus atratus*	*Cygnus olor*
Weight (kg)	4.2	4.7	5.7	10.6
(lb)	*9.2*	*10.4*	*12.6*	*23.4*
Wing length (mm)	462	427	475	588
(inches)	*18.2*	*16.8*	*18.7*	*23.1*
Tarsus length (mm)	91	85	95	109
(inches)	*3.6*	*3.3*	*3.7*	*4.3*
Mean clutch	6.8	4.5	5.1	5.8
Egg size (mm)	89 × 61	101 × 66	105 × 68	111 × 74
(inches)	*3.5 x 2.4*	*4 x 2.6*	*4.1 x 2.7*	*4.4 x 2.9*
Fresh egg weight (gm)	173	238	280	332
(oz)	*6.1*	*8.4*	*9.9*	*11.7*
Incubation period (days)	35	36	36	35.5

Scientific Name	Bewick s Swan	Whistling Swan	Whooper Swan	Trumpeter Swan
	Cygnus columbianus bewickii	*Cygnus columbianus columbianus*	*Cygnus cygnus*	*Cygnus buccinator*
Weight (kg)	6.1	6.8	9.8	11.1
(lb)	*13.4*	*15*	*21.6*	*24.5*
Wing length (mm)	521	535	596	621
(inches)	*20.5*	*21.1*	*23.5*	*24.4*
Tarsus length (mm)	104	113	118	130
(inches)	*4.1*	*4.4*	*4.6*	*5.1*
Mean clutch	3.8	4.3	4.25	5.1
Egg size (mm)	105 × 68	107 × 68	113 × 75	112 × 72
(inches)	*4.1 x 2.7*	*4.2 x 2.7*	*4.4 x 2.9*	*4.4 x 2.8*
Fresh egg weight (gm)	272	280	330	332
(oz)	*9.6*	*9.9*	*11.6*	*11.7*
Incubation period (days)	30	32	31	33

Biographical Note

Dafila Scott is a zoologist and artist, best known for her studies of birds and coral fish. She is a member of the Society of Wildlife Artists and has travelled extensively from the tropics to the Antarctic. Dafila is the daughter of ornithologist and painter Sir Peter Scott, and grand-daughter of Captain Robert Falcon Scott – 'Scott of the Antarctic'.

Recommended Reading

The Swans by Peter Scott & the Wildfowl Trust (Michael Joseph, 1972) is still the best comprehensive work describing all the species, though the population sizes and feeding habits of several species have changed in recent years. Other sources include: *The Mute Swan* by M. Birkhead and C. Perrins (Croom Helm, 1986) for a detailed account of this species; papers from the Third International Swan Symposium, published in the journal *Wildfowl*, (Supplement No.1, by WWT and IWRB) for detailed research findings; *Swans*, by Teiji Saga,(Schirmer Art Books, 1990) for a photographic celebration of whooper swans, and *A History of British Birds* (Vol. 3) by W. Yarrell, Van Doorst, (London, 1845) for a different perspective.